Sports Innovations

INNOVATIONS IN
FOOTBALL

by Douglas Hustad

SportsZone

An Imprint of Abdo Publishing
abdobooks.com

abdobooks.com

Published by Abdo Publishing, a division of ABDO, PO Box 398166, Minneapolis, Minnesota 55439. Copyright © 2022 by Abdo Consulting Group, Inc. International copyrights reserved in all countries. No part of this book may be reproduced in any form without written permission from the publisher. SportsZone™ is a trademark and logo of Abdo Publishing.

Printed in the United States of America, North Mankato, Minnesota.
102021
012022

Cover Photos: Nick Wass/AP Images, left; AP Images, right
Interior Photos: AP Images, 5, 19; Pro Football Hall of Fame/AP Images, 6, 21; Tony Tomsic/AP Images, 9; Chris Coduto/Icon Sportswire, 11; Everett Collection/Shutterstock Images, 13; Paul Spinelli/AP Images, 14, 34; Chuck Solomon/AP Images, 17; Vic Stein/ AP Images, 22; Eric Charbonneau/Invision/Sony Pictures/AP Images, 25; Matt Ludtke/AP Images, 27; Anda Chu/Bay Area News Group/Contra Costa Times/Tribune News Service/ Getty Images, 29; Ferd Kaufman/AP Images, 30–31; Matt Patterson/AP Images, 33; Ric Tapia/AP Images, 37; George Gojkovich/Getty Images Sport/Getty Images, 38; Aaron M. Sprecher/AP Images, 41; Brandon Wade/AP Images, 42–43

Editor: Katie Chanez
Series Designer: Joshua Olson

Library of Congress Control Number: 2020949104

Publisher's Cataloging-in-Publication Data

Names: Hustad, Douglas, author.
Title: Innovations in football / by Douglas Hustad
Description: Minneapolis, Minnesota : Abdo Publishing, 2022 | Series: Sports innovations | Includes online resources and index.
Identifiers: ISBN 9781532195044 (lib. bdg.) | ISBN 9781098215354 (ebook)
Subjects: LCSH: Football--Juvenile literature. | Technological innovations--Juvenile literature. | Sports sciences--Juvenile literature. | Performance technology--Juvenile literature. | Football--Equipment and supplies--Juvenile literature. | Sports-- Juvenile literature.
Classification: DDC 688.76--dc23

TABLE OF CONTENTS

CHAPTER 1

MAKING THE
MODERN NFL

Without college football, there would be no professional football. The first American football game took place between Princeton and Rutgers on November 6, 1869. But the rules were vastly different from today's game. The sport had more similarities to other games such as soccer and rugby. It wasn't until 1880 when Walter Camp devised the line of scrimmage that football began to break away and forge its own path toward becoming the game it is today.

In those early years, football was limited to colleges and other amateur teams. Then in 1892, the Allegheny Athletic Association paid William "Pudge" Heffelfinger $500 to play on its team against the rival Pittsburgh Athletic Club. That made Heffelfinger the first professional football player.

caption: **Walter Camp played on the Yale football team from 1877 to 1882.**

Soon, pro leagues started popping up around the United States. The American Professional Football Association became the dominant league after its first season in 1920. In 1922 it became the National Football League (NFL).

THE FOOLISH CLUB

Young, wealthy, and with a passion for sports, Texas businessman Lamar Hunt wanted to own an NFL team. But in the 1950s, the NFL was not interested in expanding to Hunt's

The owners of the original AFL teams called themselves "The Foolish Club."

hometown of Dallas, Texas. It would not grant him a new team, nor would it allow him to buy one and move it to Dallas. The NFL was content with its 12 established teams—two in California and the rest located in cities in the East and Midwest.

Rather than give up, Hunt decided to start his own league. Even Hunt knew it was kind of a crazy idea. He called himself and the league's first owners "The Foolish Club."

In addition to Dallas, where Hunt owned the Texans, the American Football League (AFL) brought pro football to smaller cities such as Denver, Colorado, and Buffalo, New York. Hunt formed the new league in 1959, and it began play the next year.

IN LIVING COLOR

The AFL started small but soon grew to become a true rival to the NFL. By 1962 its cumulative attendance topped 1 million fans. The AFL played an exciting style of football with plenty of passing and scoring.

ARENA FOOTBALL

Jim Foster was watching an indoor soccer game in 1981 when he had an idea. If soccer could be converted for indoor play, then football could too. Foster found a scrap of paper and started jotting down ideas for a fast-paced, high-scoring, indoor version of football. Foster started the Arena Football League in 1986, and it lasted for 30 seasons.

The NFL was more traditional, based around defense and running the ball, as it had been for decades.

The AFL's style of play excited a lot of fans. Even its appearance was exciting. Many AFL teams wore uniforms with bold, vibrant colors. The Denver Broncos wore orange. The San Diego Chargers wore powder blue and gold. These looks were perfectly timed. Football games began airing on television in color in the 1960s.

Television played a big part in the rise of the AFL. The league signed a national deal with the ABC network in 1960. This meant ABC could air AFL games on televisions nationwide. All teams shared the money the league made from the contract. That money helped teams stay in business. It also made AFL games available to a wider audience.

TIME TO MERGE

By the mid-1960s, the AFL was causing a lot of problems for the NFL. Not only was it taking fans away from the NFL, it was taking players too. In 1965 the AFL's New York Jets were able to convince quarterback Joe Namath to sign with them instead of the NFL's St. Louis Cardinals, who also had drafted him. Namath was the top college quarterback in the country after starring at the University of Alabama.

New York Jets quarterback Joe Namath was one of the first big-name college stars to sign with the AFL.

The Jets gave Namath the largest contract in pro football history. AFL teams not only had a popular league, they also had a profitable one. The AFL could compete with the NFL financially. The same year that the Jets signed Namath, the AFL signed a big television contract with NBC. The network was now able to broadcast AFL games.

The NFL had seen enough. On June 8, 1966, the AFL and NFL agreed to merge into one league. All eight AFL teams would become NFL teams starting with the 1970 season. The merger was a huge moment in football history. It created the modern NFL and also one of the biggest games in all of sports.

THE SUPER BOWL

One of the terms of the merger was to create an AFL-NFL championship game each year until the leagues officially united in 1970. There was a lot of excitement for the game. The leagues had been rivals off the field throughout the 1960s. Now they got to see how their best teams would match up on the field.

The first game was set to be called the AFL-NFL World Championship Game. But Hunt thought it should have a more unique name. "I have kiddingly called it the Super Bowl," Hunt

The Super Bowl is one of the world's biggest sporting events. The most-watched Super Bowl was Super Bowl XLIX in 2015, with 114.4 million people watching.

wrote to NFL commissioner Pete Rozelle, "which obviously can be improved upon."

And yet the name stuck. The game officially became known as the Super Bowl starting with its third edition. That year Namath led the Jets to a surprising upset of the NFL's Baltimore Colts, showing the quality of the AFL. More than 50 years later, the game is still called the Super Bowl. And it is one of the most-watched sporting events around the world each year.

CHAPTER **2**

AIRING IT OUT

Many rule changes helped create the modern game of football. But few had as big of an impact as the forward pass. Until 1906, players could only pitch the ball backward, as they do in rugby. Whoever received the ball then could run with it until he was tackled or passed it backward again.

Part of the reason forward passing was made legal was safety. Football had become a violent and bloody game. In 1905, 18 players were killed in college games across the country. Many colleges were threatening to ban the sport until President Theodore Roosevelt stepped in. He worked with college presidents to make the game safer.

The forward pass would help open up the game and avoid the gang tackles that led to injuries. But many early coaches still resisted using the forward pass. They saw it as being weak and against the spirit of football.

caption: **President Theodore Roosevelt wanted football to be safer.**

The forward pass has created many dramatic moments in football, including toe-tap touchdowns.

One man who saw the potential was Glenn Scobey "Pop" Warner. Warner was the coach at Carlisle Indian Industrial School in Pennsylvania. The forward pass helped Warner make Carlisle one of the top college football teams of the 1900s. Warner invented a formation in which the ball carrier could run, pass, or kick. The defense had a hard time preparing for all of those options. Carlisle was able to complete almost any pass it wanted.

THE PASS POTENTIAL

Passing was still limited compared to today. The passer had to be at least five yards behind the line of scrimmage when he threw the ball. If he wasn't, the ball turned over to the defense. The referee had to make this judgment.

In 1932 the Chicago Bears were playing the Plymouth Spartans in a playoff game. The Bears had a future Hall of Famer on their team in Bronko Nagurski. Nagurski was responsible for the winning score when he faked a run before throwing a touchdown pass.

THE PROLATE SPHEROID

Footballs were round in the early days of the game. Once passing became common, the ball was redesigned for throwing. Hugh "Shorty" Ray is credited as the man who designed the modern football shape. This shape is known as a prolate spheroid.

The Spartans players insisted Nagurski was not five yards behind the line. But the play stood, and the Bears won 9–0. The next year, the NFL made passes legal anywhere behind the line of scrimmage. Spartans coach George "Potsy" Clark was actually one of the people who argued for the rule change. Why? "Because Nagurski will do it anyway," he said.

"AIR CORYELL"

Despite these changes to increase passing, the NFL was still mostly a running league. Teams usually used a pro set formation on offense. This included two wide receivers, one tight end, and two running backs.

A couple of important changes took place in the NFL in 1978. A new rule made it illegal for defenders to make significant contact with a receiver more than five yards past the line of scrimmage. The league also loosened the rules for linemen to help them block for their quarterback.

Additionally, in 1978 Don Coryell became head coach of the San Diego Chargers. Coryell removed a running back from the pro set offense. He then added a second tight end who could catch well. In the Chargers' case, this was future Hall of Famer Kellen Winslow. Coryell frequently deployed three- and four-receiver sets and passed the ball often.

His offense became known as "Air Coryell." The Chargers led the NFL in passing yards every year from 1978 to 1983. Dan Fouts became a Hall of Fame quarterback. And the rest of the NFL raced to catch up.

San Diego Chargers coach Don Coryell, *center*, helped promote passing in the NFL.

THE WEST COAST OFFENSE

In 1985 the New York Giants faced off against the San Francisco 49ers in the playoffs. Giants coach Bill Parcells relied on defense and a rushing attack to win. Bill Walsh and the 49ers used a quick passing attack. After the Giants snuffed out the 49ers' passing in a 17–3 win, Parcells said, "What do you think of that West Coast offense now?"

But Walsh would have the last laugh. Using the West Coast offense, he guided the 49ers to three Super Bowl wins in the 1980s. Walsh's offense was hard for defenses to understand. He often changed how it looked and used multiple wide receivers. Like Air Coryell, Walsh's offensive strategy was copied throughout the NFL.

Many modern NFL teams still use versions of the West Coast offense. But other unique systems also are popular. Coaches continue to innovate to give their team an edge.

From left, 49ers head coach Bill Walsh, quarterback Joe Montana, and team owner Edward DeBartolo, Jr., celebrate after winning the Super Bowl in January 1985.

CHAPTER 3

SAFETY FIRST

Even modern football helmets can't fully protect players from head injuries. But for decades, players didn't wear helmets at all. And once they did start wearing helmets, the head gear didn't offer much protection.

One of the first players to wear a helmet was Navy player Joseph Reeves in 1893. Reeves had taken so many hits to the head a doctor warned him he could suffer permanent damage with just one more hit. Not wanting to miss the rivalry game against Army, Reeves wore a hat with earflaps made out of fabric.

In the early days, helmets were more like caps than the helmets of today. They were made of leather with padding inside. They were very hot, and the earflaps made it hard to hear. Helmets were optional in the NFL until 1943.

caption: **Early football helmets didn't offer the same level of protection as modern ones.**

The Los Angeles Rams were the first NFL team to put their logo on their helmets, displayed here by Hall of Fame wide receiver Tom Fears.

PLASTIC HELMETS

In 1922 John T. Riddell invented the removable football cleat. It was so successful among his players at Evanston Township High School near Chicago that he started his own sporting goods company. He kept inventing new equipment too. In 1939 Riddell devised the first plastic football helmet.

Early plastic shattered easily. The NFL banned plastic helmets at first but soon brought them back. Over the years, helmets added padding, face masks, and other features of the modern helmet. Los Angeles Rams running back Fred Gehrke painted horns on his helmet in 1948, making the Rams the first NFL team with a helmet logo.

The Riddell company continued to make most of the helmets used in the NFL. In 2002 it announced a major redesign for safety. The Revolution model helmet was designed to reduce concussions.

Today the NFL has a testing standard for helmets. Helmets must pass in order to be safe enough to use on the field.

THE MASKLESS MAN

In 1955 the NFL mandated that helmets had to have face masks. Players had to get special permission to play without one. One of these players was defensive end Tommy McDonald. McDonald was the last non-kicker to play without a face mask. He retired after the 1968 season.

Helmets that don't pass or that are too old are banned from use in the league.

MINIMIZING CONCUSSIONS

In 2002 Dr. Bennet Omalu was working as a medical examiner in Pittsburgh. He was assigned to examine the body of Mike Webster, a former NFL player who had died of a heart attack. Omalu noticed Webster's brain showed signs of a disease Omalu called chronic traumatic encephalopathy (CTE). This disease normally affected boxers, who took frequent blows to the head as part of their job.

Omalu's findings prompted more research into head injuries in the NFL. Researchers began examining the brains of deceased NFL players for CTE. They discovered the disease was widespread.

In 2009 the NFL announced a series of protocols to help protect players with concussions. Trained professionals are on-site at games to identify players who may have suffered a head injury. The players are then pulled from the game and evaluated. Players who are found to be potentially concussed are not allowed to re-enter the game.

Dr. Bennet Omalu's work to raise awareness about CTE in football players was made into a 2015 movie called *Concussion*.

SAFETY RULES

Ever since colleges nearly banned football in 1905 because it was too dangerous, people have tried to make the sport safer. Football is a physical and violent sport. It will never be truly safe. But the NFL and other leagues have used rule changes to attempt to reduce injuries.

One of the most dangerous plays in football is the kickoff. Players from both teams are running at each other at full speed before they collide violently. The NFL banned running starts on kickoffs in 2018. That means players on the kicking team must line up no more than one yard behind the ball and cannot leave until the ball is kicked. This limits those players' opportunity to build up speed as they run downfield to cover the return. That reduces the impact on collisions. The NFL reported a 35 percent reduction in concussions on kickoff plays from 2017.

All levels of play have issued strict punishments for hits to the head. In college football, targeting is called when a player intentionally hits another player in the head. The play is subject to review. If officials confirm targeting, they eject the offending player from the game. If targeting happens in the second half of a game, the player then also misses the first half of his team's next game.

Rule changes have been implemented in an effort to increase player safety.

In the NFL, players can be ejected for helmet-to-helmet hits that injure their opponents. Players are also coached to avoid tackling this way.

CHAPTER 4

FOR THE FANS

In fantasy football, owners accumulate points based on how the players on their team perform in real life. Bill "Wink" Winkenbach didn't need to play fantasy football. He had managed a real team as an owner of the Oakland Raiders. But in 1962, he invented a game that allowed fans to manage their own custom-built NFL teams.

Winkenbach came up with fantasy football during a Raiders road trip to New York. He held the first ever draft in his home in 1963. The first player taken was Houston Oilers quarterback George Blanda. That first fantasy league, the Greater Oakland Professional Pigskin Prognosticators League, was still going strong more than 50 years later. By then they were joined by millions of other participants around the world.

Fantasy football exploded in popularity in the 1990s. As more people gained access to the internet, it became easier

caption:

Early fantasy football leagues were all done by hand. Some leagues still draft fantasy teams on paper.

Fans loved attending games at the Cotton Bowl in Dallas, Texas.

to create and host leagues. Rather than keep stats manually, internet sites offered stats tracking for free. People could watch highlights of their fantasy players on popular shows such as ESPN's *SportsCenter*.

Today, fantasy football is big business. Approximately 60 million people play in the United States and Canada each year. Stadiums display fantasy stats so fantasy players can

track their teams at games. TV networks show the stats right alongside that day's NFL scores. For many participants, fantasy football is just as exciting as the real thing.

PALACES OF FOOTBALL

In the 1960s, most football stadiums were very simple. They were designed just for watching a game and did not have many other amenities for fans. The Cotton Bowl in Dallas was no different. The home of the Cowboys was a basic concrete bowl.

Cowboys owner Clint Murchison wanted something better for his fans. He promised them the finest football stadium in the world.

Texas Stadium opened in 1971. It was one of the first stadiums to feature luxury boxes. These suites made a lot of money for the Cowboys. But some of the new perks were designed for regular fans, too. The stadium featured its own restaurant and had TVs in the concourse. A roof covered fans but was open above the playing field. That kept fans dry during rainy games.

Texas Stadium was the first modern NFL stadium. Stadiums today feature lots of amenities for fans to enjoy. Some feature retractable roofs to protect fans from the elements. Some have stadium clubs for fans to gather in before games. They feature huge video boards for the best replays and information. Attending an NFL game today is a far different experience than it was before Murchison's vision became reality.

INTERNATIONAL SERIES

In 2005 Mexico City hosted the first NFL regular-season game outside of the United States. In 2007 the NFL scheduled a game in London, England. Through 2019 the league played at least one game in London every year. The NFL has also considered playing games in China and Germany to keep growing its international fanbase.

Reliant Stadium in Houston was the first NFL stadium to feature a retractable roof.

MONDAY NIGHT FOOTBALL

In 1969 NFL commissioner Pete Rozelle wanted to expand when games were played. Previously, NFL games were only played on Sunday afternoon. However, the NFL could not play games on Fridays because it did not want to interfere with high school football. Saturdays were reserved for college football. But Monday night was wide open. The NFL could stage a game on Monday night and have the audience all to itself.

Monday Night Football moved to ESPN for the start of the 2006 season. Its pregame show is called *Monday Night Countdown.*

Rozelle needed a partner. He pitched the idea to CBS and NBC, but both networks turned him down. Their schedules were tied up with established programming. But ABC's schedule needed a boost. ABC Sports president Roone Arledge loved the idea. He agreed to a three-year contract starting in 1970.

The figures in the broadcast booth were almost as important to the Monday night broadcasts as the games themselves. Arledge hired controversial New York broadcaster Howard Cosell and charismatic former Cowboys quarterback Don Meredith to provide analysis. In 1971 Arledge added popular former New York Giants player Frank Gifford to the crew.

Monday Night Football used more camera angles and more replays than regular NFL broadcasts. The technology and the mix of personalities was like nothing fans had ever seen. And they loved it. Within a year, *Monday Night Football* was drawing 30 million viewers per week. Ongoing as of 2020, it is one of the longest-running prime time shows in US television history.

CHAPTER 5

USING
TECHNOLOGY

As fans started to see replays of key moments in the games at home thanks to television, the NFL began to look at ways to use instant replay during games. In 1976 NFL director of officiating Art McNally took a stopwatch and a video camera up to the press box at Texas Stadium. McNally timed how long it would take to review a play by video. He also saw one controversial play that could have been overturned had the league been using instant replay. McNally knew the NFL needed to make a change.

The league tested an instant replay system in the 1978 preseason. But the system was expensive to install, took too long to review, and did not offer enough angles to properly review plays. The NFL tried again in 1985. But there were more glitches. Replay vanished again in 1992.

caption: **Instant replay has become a key tool of officials in NFL games.**

Earlier versions of instant replay used a sideline display that allowed officials to review video footage.

Still, coaches, owners, and the league never stopped debating it. An improved system returned for the 1999 season, and replay has remained part of the NFL ever since. The league has taken steps to speed up reviews and make them more accurate. From a peak of just over three minutes in 2004, reviews took an average of 2 minutes, 8 seconds in 2019.

NFL referees now view plays on the sideline using league-issued tablets. The league also has a central review office in New York where officials help referees review plays. That office is called Art McNally GameDay Central.

THE FIRST-DOWN LINE

Fans in the stands never have to wonder where the first-down line is. They can just look over to the handheld marker on the sideline. But TV viewers didn't have that option. That all changed in 1998.

THE FIRST TV GAME

The Super Bowl today draws about 100 million viewers. The first NFL game on TV drew about 1,000. The Philadelphia Eagles and Brooklyn Dodgers squared off in the first televised NFL game on October 22, 1939. It was only aired in New York City. The broadcast featured only two camera angles, no replays, and just one broadcaster.

An inventor named David Crain had the idea for a visual first down line on TV broadcasts in 1976. But the networks did not have the necessary technology. The idea was revived in 1998. A company called Sportvision developed a way to project a yellow line onto the field. Called 1st and Ten, the system debuted in a game between the Baltimore Ravens and Cincinnati Bengals on September 27, 1998.

Almost every football game on TV today features the 1st and Ten line. Broadcasters haven't stopped innovating on-field graphics either. Now they use technology to project other useful information like the down and distance, highlight individual players, and even project play diagrams.

SKYCAM

Inventor Garrett Brown is best known as the inventor of the Steadicam. The Steadicam revolutionized the film industry. It steadies the camera so that it does not shake as it is carried. Brown is also the inventor of SkyCam. SkyCam gave fans a perspective they hadn't seen. It flies above the action on wires.

SkyCam debuted in the NFL in 1984. At the time it was rarely used because it was very expensive to operate. It didn't become a regular feature in broadcasts until 2001. A new football league called the XFL kicked off that season and used SkyCam for all its games.

The XFL only lasted one season. But the SkyCam stayed. It is now in use in most televised football games. It has also even

SkyCam uses wires to travel above the field, where a handheld camera can't go.

The XFL was revived in 2020, but the first season was cut short due to the COVID-19 pandemic. The league filed for bankruptcy and was purchased by a group headed by Dwayne "the Rock" Johnson.

spread to other sports such as soccer and auto racing. Some games have even been broadcast using SkyCam as the main camera angle.

All these technological innovations have helped the NFL become one of the most-watched sports leagues in the world. But it would not be so popular without the many on-field innovations as well. Football is a totally different sport from the game that was first played way back in 1869.

TIMELINE

1869
The first college football game takes place between Princeton and Rutgers.

1892
William "Pudge" Heffelfinger becomes the first pro football player when he earns $500 to play for Allegheny Athletic Club.

1906
The forward pass is legalized in football.

1939
John T. Riddell invents the plastic football helmet, which soon becomes the standard in the NFL.

1963
Bill Winkenbach holds the first fantasy football draft in Oakland, California.

1966
The AFL and NFL agree to merge, forming the basis of the modern NFL.

1970
ABC begins airing *Monday Night Football*, the first weekly weeknight game on the NFL schedule.

1976
The NFL begins experimenting with instant replay to review controversial plays.

1998
The 1st and Ten visual first down line becomes a common feature of football broadcasts.

2009
The NFL institutes concussion protocol to minimize the risk of brain injuries.

HONORABLE MENTIONS

FIELDTURF

Football damages grass. But artificial turf also damages skin and offers no natural cushioning. FieldTurf solved all of these problems. First used in the NFL in 2002, FieldTurf combines artificial grass with a soft base of rubber. FieldTurf performs similarly to real grass but is much more durable. Most NFL stadiums use FieldTurf or similar products.

IN-HELMET COMMUNICATIONS

In 1956 a pair of Ohio inventors approached Cleveland Browns coach Paul Brown with an idea. They had devised a small radio transmitter that Brown could use to talk to his players on the field. When Brown deployed the system in a preseason game against the Detroit Lions, the Lions were suspicious. They spotted the system on the sideline, and it was soon banned. The NFL legalized in-helmet communications in 1994.

DETERMINING THE COLLEGE CHAMPION

For a long time, there wasn't an on-field system to determine a college football champion. Instead, different groups of people voted. The top-ranked team was considered the champion. But there were multiple polls, and they didn't always agree. The Bowl Championship Series (BCS) used both polls and computer rankings. The BCS was first used in 1998 to determine which teams should face off for the national title. But the BCS was controversial, too, because it left some teams out. It was replaced by the College Football Playoff in 2014.

GLOSSARY

amateur
A person who plays a sport without getting paid.

ban
To stop something from being used or performed for a period of time.

commissioner
The chief executive of a sports league.

concussion
A traumatic brain injury caused by a blow to the head.

ejected
Removed from a game, usually due to unsportsmanlike behavior.

line of scrimmage
The place on the field where a play starts.

playoffs
A set of games played after the regular season that decides which team is the champion.

preseason
Games before the regular season that are used as practice and don't count toward the standings.

press box
An area in a stadium reserved for reporters to do their work.

professional
A person who gets paid to perform.

rival
An opponent with whom a player or team has a fierce and ongoing competition.

BOOKS

Wilner, Barry. *Great Football Debates*. Minneapolis, MN: Abdo Publishing, 2019.

Wilner, Barry. *Total Football*. Minneapolis, MN: Abdo Publishing, 2017.

York, Andy. *Ultimate College Football Road Trip*. Minneapolis, MN:
    Abdo Publishing, 2019.

ONLINE RESOURCES

To learn more about innovations in football, please visit
abdobooklinks.com or scan this QR code. These links are
routinely monitored and updated to provide the most current
information available.

INDEX

ABOUT THE AUTHOR

Douglas Hustad is a freelance author primarily of science and history books for young people. He, his wife, and their two dogs live in the northern suburbs of San Diego, California.